Snappy Critters
Easy-to-Make
Plush Toys

VOID

Ted Menter

DOVER PUBLICATIONS, INC.
Mineola, New York

WARNING: Children should only do the projects described in this book under adult supervision. The projects require working with pins and small objects, such as beads and snaps, that pose dangers and are potential choking hazards for small children.

CONTENTS

Welcome to Snappyville

At the edge of the green woods and across the pond from cliffs of the great mountain is the tiny village of Snappyville.

The inhabitants of this community call themselves "the Snappys" because they are all very different but are all created the same way—just like human beings!

Here in Snappyville there are all sorts of plush critters who often have brothers and sisters as well as cousins.

There are Betty and Bobby Bunny who love to eat carrots and hide colorful eggs at Easter time. Down the lane is Karol Kitty and her cousin Tilly Tiger. In the tiny house with blue shutters lives Martin Mouse and across the street is the large white house of his neighbor Leonard Lion.

The Snappys love to play together and celebrate all the holidays. They make valentines, shamrocks, and Christmas stockings as well as delightful Easter eggs.

Some of the Snappys wear plaid outfits while others wear scarves or circus ruffs around their necks.

Snappyville is full of fun and fantasy just waiting to be explored. All it takes is some imagination plus a needle and thread.

What is a Snappy?

A Snappy is an easy-to-make jointed stuffed toy animal. Each Snappy is about seven inches tall not counting their ears. They are called Snappys because their joints are made with dressmaker snaps.

A Snappy can be made from almost any fabric, from expensive mohair to inexpensive terry cloth. And, of course, there are the four "F" materials—fur, felt, flannel, and fleece. All of these fabrics will be discussed in a later chapter.

The techniques used to make a Snappy are quick and easy but might be unfamiliar to sewers who have never made a stuffed toy before or are accustomed to the more traditional techniques. There are illustrated step-by-step instructions with photographs that explain, in detail, each step in the process.

There are almost endless possibilities for creating your own unique Snappy companion. They are a fun project for schools, as well as doll and teddy bear clubs. I taught a Snappy class online to over 200 students worldwide and a delightful time was had by all the students. That class was the inspiration for this book.

Fabric Personalities

When you are ready to create your first Snappy it is important to consider what sort of animal it will be based on and what fabric will work best to express that critter's persona.

FLEECE has become a very popular fabric for making toy animals. It is soft and dense and very easy to sew.

HEAVY WOOL and FLANNEL offer a similar effect to fleece but the surface is not as fuzzy.

FELT is easy to sew and can be wire brushed to add texture to the surface.

MOHAIR is the traditional fabric used for over a hundred years to create plush toys. It is a bit more expensive than the other fabrics.

Fun Fabrics for a Snappy

There are many fabrics that can be used to create a delightful Snappy Critter. Basically, there are two categories—woven and non-woven. For instance, mohair fabric is a woven fabric. Fleece and flannel would fall into the non-woven category because they generally have a stretch quality that needs to be stabilized. Felt needs to be stabilized because it can stretch and has the potential to weaken and split apart. Lightweight cottons need to be stabilized for added strength.

In order to stabilize fabrics it is necessary to back them with lightweight WOVEN iron-on interfacing.

It is ESSENTIAL that it be a woven interfacing in order for it to stabilize a fabric. A non-woven interfacing will not stabilize a fabric that stretches when it is stuffed.

The iron-on woven interfacing is available in most fabric shops. And it has a secondary function. It provides a clean surface to trace out your patterns.

Certain fabrics, like fleece and terry cloth are the same on both sides so the iron-on woven interfacing helps to flatten the back and makes a stable surface to trace out the patterns.

Most of the time, mohair with a light color backing does not require any interfacing. However, if the backing is a dark color then it is best to use the interfacing as a light surface to trace out the patterns.

Picking a Fabric

Many types of fabric can be used to make a Snappy. There are also animal print fabrics available, but the trick is to find a print in the right scale. Later on we will discuss how to create animal prints if you cannot find one in the right scale and colors.

There are several major differences between faux fur and mohair, and basic fuzzy fabrics like fleece and terry cloth. Here are a few tips for working with mohair:

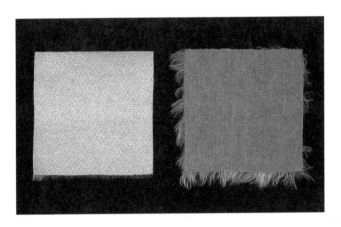

Looking at these two swatches from the back it is hard to see the fur direction.

Looking at the swatches from the front does not show much direction either.

If you fold the swatch from top to bottom you can see that the fur tends to stand straight out.

If you fold the swatch from side to side you can see that the fur tends to lay in a downward direction.

Supplies & Tools

This is a list of supplies needed to make a Snappy:

- Plush fabric or mohair
- Woven interfacing
- Felt for ear lining
- Pom-poms
- Dress snaps #1 or #2
- Tiny 1/8-inch beads for eyes
- Fiber-fill for stuffing
- Pipe cleaner for tails

This is a list of tools needed to make a Snappy:

- Scissors
- Needle-nose pliers
- Screwdriver
- Bamboo skewer
- Forceps
- Permanent markers
- Sewing thread
- Carpet thread
- Fabric glue
- Round head pins

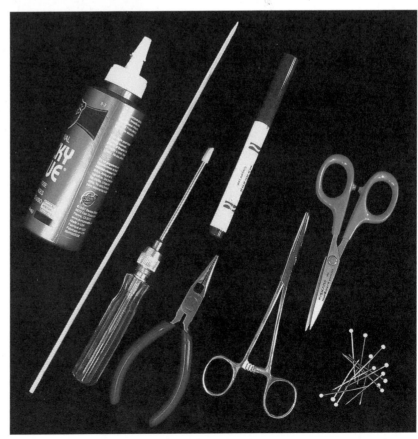

Pick a Pattern

Will your Snappy be a bunny or a bear? When you have decided which critter will be your first creation it is time to select the pattern. If you have a computer scanner then it is easy to scan, copy, and print out the pattern of your choice. Or, you can make a copy at your local print shop. You can always just trace the patterns and transfer them to card stock. It is important to use medium-weight paper stock for printing the patterns or you can mount them on manila file folders, which make excellent pattern backing.

Another of the ESSENTIALS is carefully tracing the patterns onto the back of your fabric because this will be your sewing line.

Profile Patterns

A profile pattern has a couple of advantages. They are easy to sew, can be enlarged or reduced, and will remain in the correct proportion with no distortion.

All of the Snappy patterns, including their accessories, are profile patterns. Like the magical "one size fits all" garment, profile patterns work for every Snappy.

This profile pattern and sewing technique might be new to some crafters. But once you have tried it and created your first Snappy, it will be much easier the second time.

Just read the directions, look at the photos, and have fun!

Sewing Snappy

Each Snappy Critter is made from two pieces of fur or fabric. Be sure that if you are using a fabric like fleece or terry cloth that you back it first. The average Snappy uses two pieces of fabric about 15 inches long and 5 inches wide. Always test your pattern layout on a piece of paper first.

Be sure that you mark the joint "dots" on the back of your fabric.

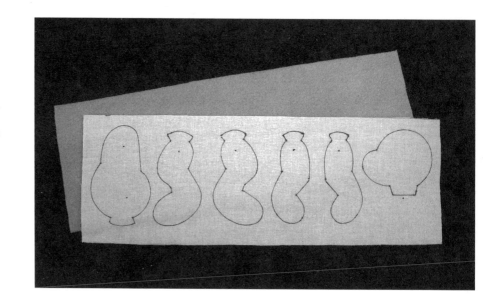

With dark thread create a knot where each of the snap joints will be located. This is important because it will make certain that your Snappy's arms and legs are evenly spaced.

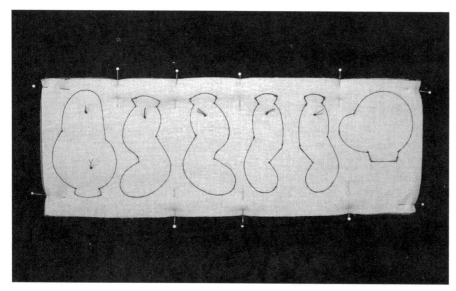

It will be necessary to create the knots of the other side of the body, but that can be done later.

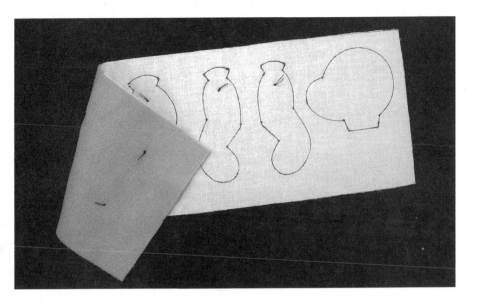

The next step will be to pin the two strips of fabric together—furry sides of fabric face to face. Be sure to pin the pieces securely enough to avoid the bottom piece from slipping when you are sewing. You will notice that each pattern piece has a top flap. This flap indicates two things: an opening for stuffing and the beginning and ending of your sewing. Remember that your pattern outline is your sewing line.

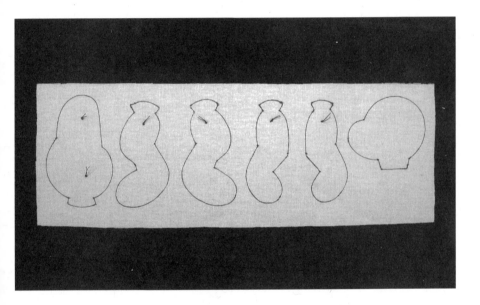

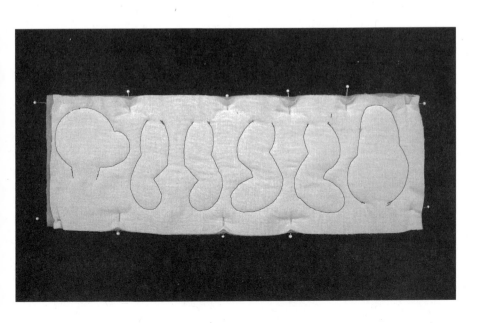

When you turn the sewn pieces over, you will see that the sewn outline appears on both sides.

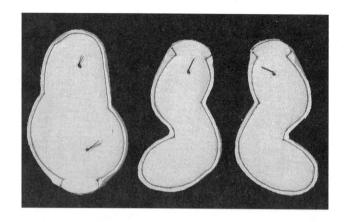

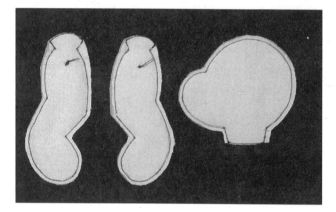

Cutting Out the Pieces

Cutting out the pieces is an easy task if you have used a fabric like fleece or felt. Since you have only drawn the pattern on one side of the fabric, that is the side that should be facing up when you cut. The tops of the arms and legs have a 1/4 inch seam allowance, but since the Snappy is a rather small critter it is best to cut the rest of the seam allowance to about 1/8 inch. This will make turning out the pieces much easier. While the Snappy ears are included in these two sample layouts they are usually made later.

Cutting Fur Fabric

If you have never worked with fur fabric, either Mohair or synthetic, you need to learn how to cut fur fabric correctly. Basically, it is important to only cut the backing—not the fur itself. Simply insert your scissors carefully under the fur and cut just the backing. Cut one side at a time. When you finish cutting, pull the pieces apart and you should be able to see bits of fur showing outside the cutting line.

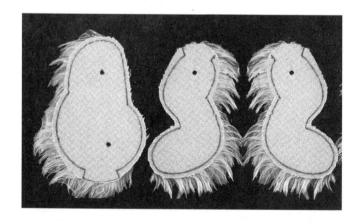

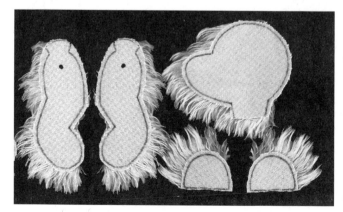

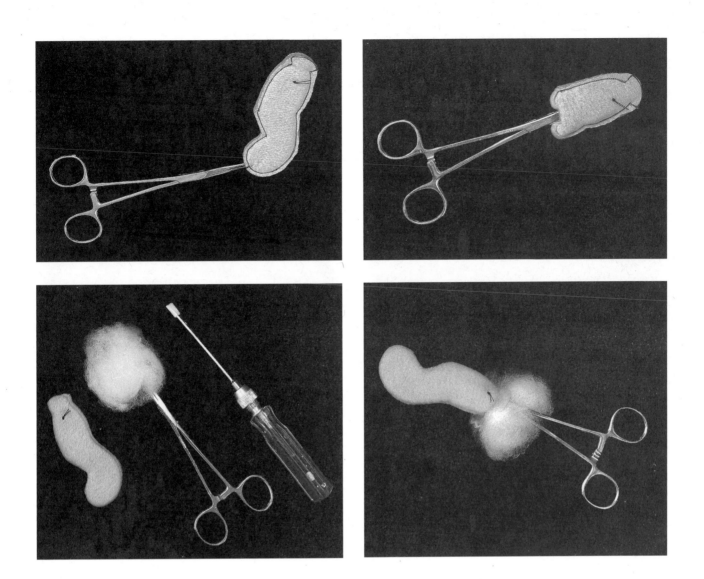

Stuffing Snappy

Stuffing the Snappy is made much easier with the use of two common tools—forceps (also called hemostats) and a slim screwdriver with the tip covered in tape to soften the edges.

Use the forceps to grab the tip of a sewn piece and push it inside itself to turn the piece right side out.

Next, use the forceps to push the stuffing into the head and body pieces. Then use the screwdriver to pack the stuffing tightly inside the piece. Try to stuff your Snappy as firmly as possible.

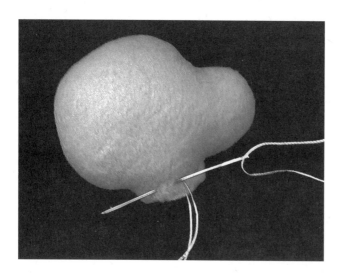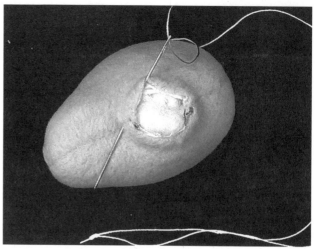

Closing the Snappy Head

After you have firmly stuffed the head of your Snappy it is time to close it up. Take a length of carpet thread—about 15 inches—and thread a needle. Then make a fat knot at the end of the thread. Begin by inserting the needle inside the neck (actually the extended seam allowance) by the seam under the chin. Your sewing line should be 1/4 inch up from the bottom edge of the neck. Next, use a running stitch around the neck with stitches about 1/8 inch apart. Pull the thread to gather the neck together. Be sure to tuck the seam allowance inside the head so that your closure is smooth and tight. Finish by sewing a lock stitch to keep the gather together. Now, using the same thread, you can sew on the bottom half of the snap directly over the center of the gather.

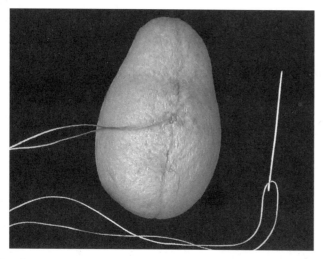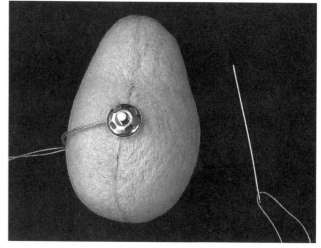

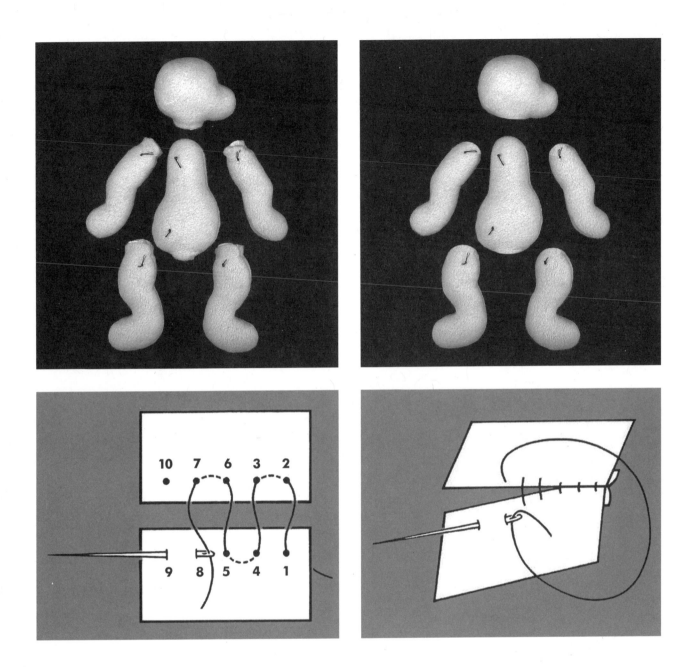

The Ladder Stitch

The ladder stitch is essential in making a Snappy. Use carpet thread to close the Snappy parts. Start with a fat knot inside one end of the opening to be closed. Now, working from side to side, keep thinking in-out, cross over, in-out, cross over *(see illustration)*. Your stitches should be about 1/8 inch long with the same amount of space between the stitches. Make sure the seam allowance folds under and disappears inside behind the closing. When you have finished the stitches you can pull the thread tight and create a locking stitch at the end.

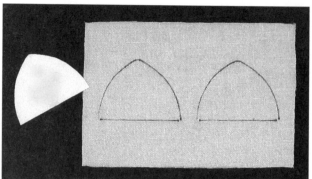

Ears

All of the Snappys have ears, but they vary from critter to critter. However, the technique for making the ears and sewing them onto the head is the same regardless of the ear shape.

The back of the ear should be made of the same material as the body. The inside of the ear can be made of lightweight felt in a different color or from lightweight fabric.

Trace the pattern onto the back of the fabric that has iron-on woven interfacing. Pin that fabric to the felt or fabric that is being used for the inside of the ear. Sew the ears, but leave the bottom edge open. Be sure to always backstitch the start and finish of your sewing.

Trim away the seam allowance and turn out the ear. Use a few drops of glue to close the bottom edge together.

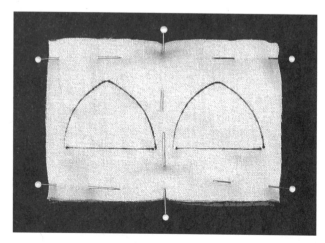
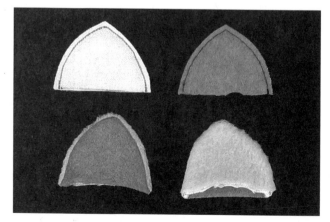

Pin the center of the ear to the side of the Snappy head.

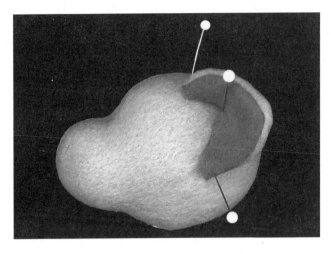

Fold the two ends forward and pin them in position.

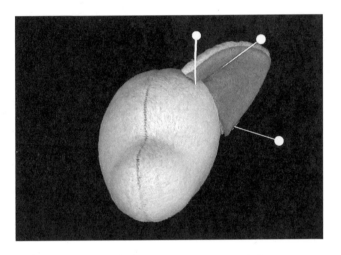

You can now see the ear is shaped the way you want.

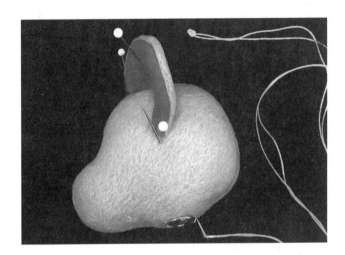

Starting at one end of the ear, sew the ear in place.

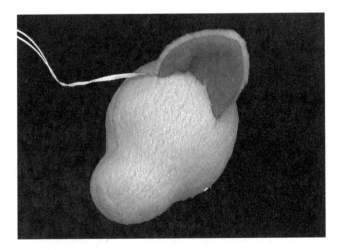

Catch the bottom edge with small stitches.

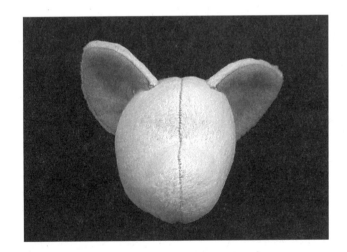

Repeat the process to position and sew the other ear.

Nose & Cheeks

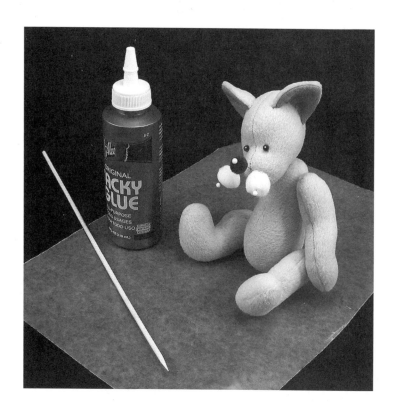

This is the fun part of making a Snappy—creating a face. The basics are pretty simple because the nose and cheeks are made from fuzzy pom-poms. You can create different expressions by using large or small pom-poms, as well as light and dark colors.

Always work on wax paper when using fabric glue as it keeps the glue from drying out.

Use black round head pins to indicate the eyes. Then pin the nose and cheeks into position.

When you have the expression you want then pull the pom-poms away from the face so you have room to apply the glue.

Use a toothpick or a bamboo skewer to apply glue under the nose and cheeks. Push the nose and cheeks down onto the face and let dry.

Mark eye position with round head pins.

Eyes

Where you place the eyes in a Snappy head can change the expression of the critter. Begin by testing the position with two round head pins. As luck would have it, these pin heads are about the same size as 1/8 inch beads that will be the Snappy's final eyes. Once you have set the eyes you can thread the beads and sew them onto the head. The best way to do this is to push a long needle through the head coming out by the snap under the chin. Do the same with the other eye and the second threads coming out next to the first. Tie the threads together to secure the eyes and bury the thread tails inside the head.

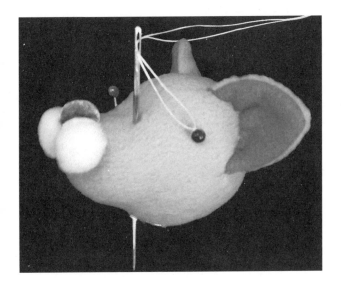

Insert needle through head.

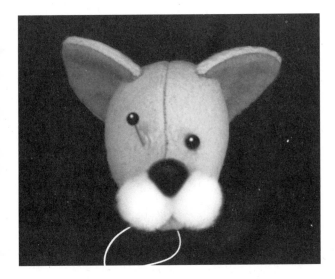

Pull thread and eye through.

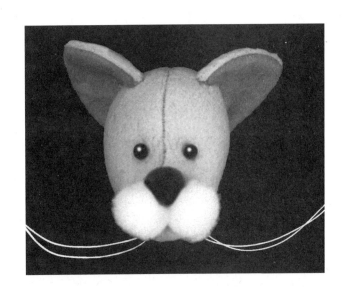

Knot the threads and bury inside head.

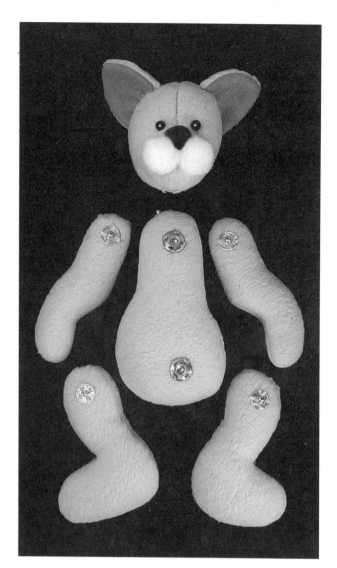

Jointing Snappy

The Snappy Critter is jointed using dressmaker metal snaps. Snaps come in two parts. The top part has the nub and the bottom part has the opening to grip it. Your Snappy is jointed by using the top part sewn onto the arms and legs. The bottom part of the snap is sewn onto the body.

The head has the bottom part of the snap sewn onto the center of the head closing. The top part of the snap is sewn to the top of the body.

The knots you tied indicate placement of the snaps. To help position your snaps, put a pin through the center of the snap parts to hold the snap securely while sewing it in place.

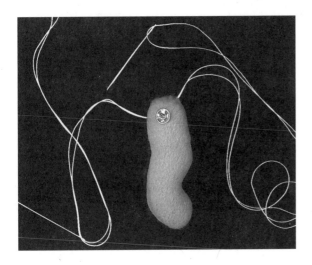
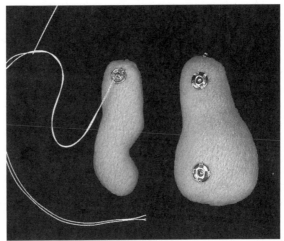

Permanent Snappy Joints

The Snappys are lots of fun to play with, but some folks prefer not to have the arms and legs snap apart all the time.

Here is a simple way to secure the joints without losing any mobility: After you close the top (stuffing) opening on the arms and legs you can make a slight change in the process of attaching the snap. Instead of attaching the top snap with the closing thread, insert the needle through the center hole of the snap. Next, thread a second needle and sew the snap in place. Take the needle and thread from the center of the snap and insert it into the center hole of the bottom snap in the body. Pull the thread through the body coming out on the far side of the opposing side snap. Snap the joint together, pull the thread tight and secure it with a locking knot. Now your joint is secure and the arms and legs will not pop off during play.

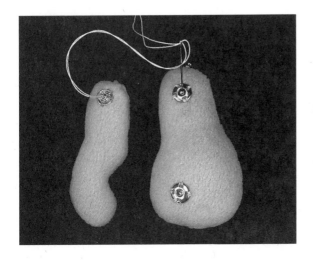
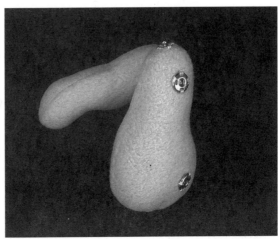

Let's Make a Two-Tone Snappy

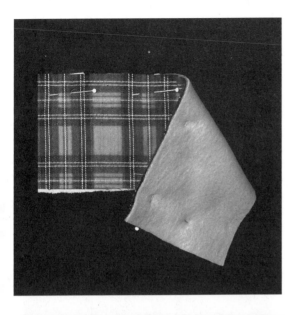

Some of the Snappys like to dress up, and this is one way to create the appearance of a dressed Snappy. Begin with two pieces of fabric. In this example, a plaid fabric and a piece of plush fabric that is the same as the fabric to be used for the head. Sew the two pieces together along the longest side and trim back the seam allowance to about 1/8 inch. Iron the two pieces flat and then back them with iron-on woven interfacing. Place the arm and leg patterns so that the seam of the two fabrics is on the wrist and ankle. This will make the arms and legs to appear to have cuffs.

Cut out the pieces the same way as an all plush version. Turn out the pieces and stuff them. The body will be made entirely of the plaid fabric and can have buttons and a ruff to complete the outfit.

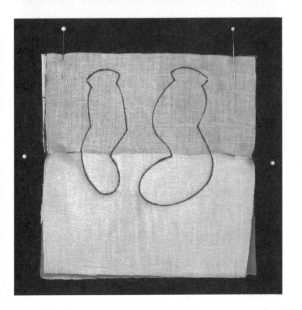

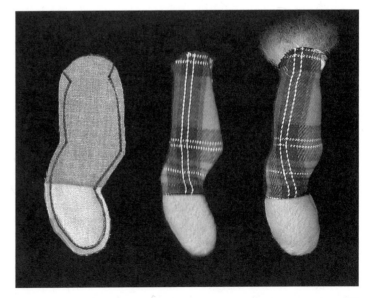

Two-Tone Snappys

There are several ways to create a two-tone Snappy. You can use different fabrics like in the Panda or create two tones with paint or appliqué. You can cut out shapes like the puppy's spots and glue them in place. Or, use fabric markers to create a blended look like in the Siamese cat or stripes on the tiger.

Heads & Tails

Many of the Snappys have a tail and some of them have more hair on their heads, like Lenny Lion and Sammy Squirrel. Giving a Snappy a tail can be fun and challenging. Making a mane for Lenny Lion is not as difficult as it might look. There are a few tricks to creating certain hair pieces.

Creating tails can be fun and will add personality to your Snappy!

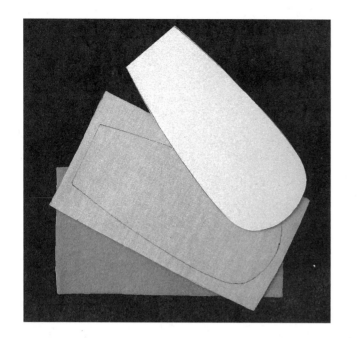

Squirrel Tail

Many of the Snappy Critters have long tails or cottontails like the bunny.

A squirrel (or a beaver) has a wide tail that curls. This tail is really quite easy to create. Trace out the pattern on the back of one piece of fur or fabric.

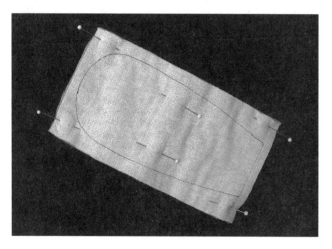

Pin the fur fabric together fur-to-fur. Sew together leaving the bottom open.

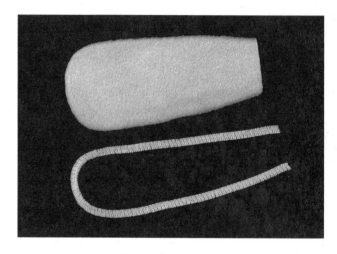

Trim the seam allowance and turn out. Apply fabric glue along the pipe cleaner.

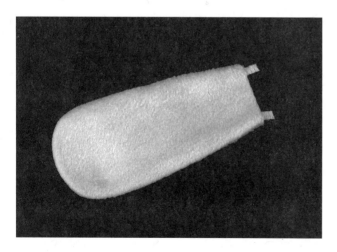

Insert pipe cleaner and push the edges along the sides of the tail. Trim excess.

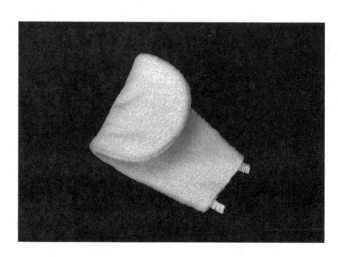

Sew finished tail to the backside of the Snappy as you did the ears.

Cat Tail

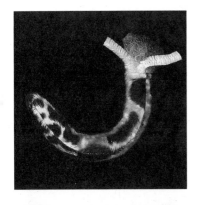

Many of the Snappys have long tails. A mouse has a slim tail and a cat has a thicker tail. The straight tail can either be lightly stuffed or have a pipe cleaner inserted to add shape. After you insert the pipe cleaner, or finish the stuffing, you can trim off any excess and sew the tail to Snappy's backside using the same technique as sewing on the ears.

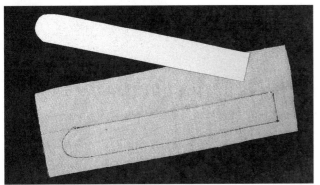

Layout the pattern on half the fabric.

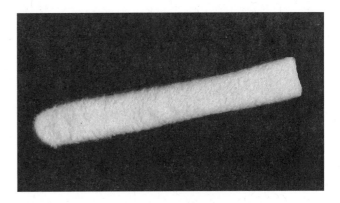

Fold the fabric along one side.

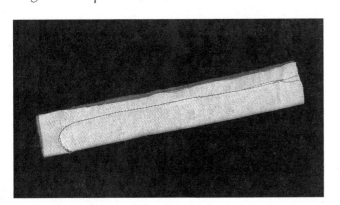

Sew the seam leaving the end open.

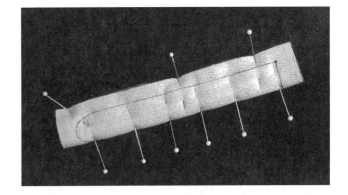

Trim seam allowance and turn out.

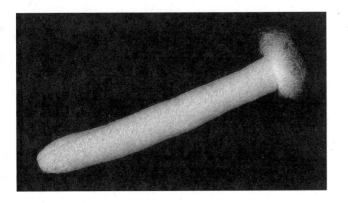

Lightly stuff the tail.

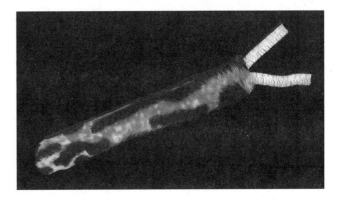

Insert a pipe cleaner to add shape.

Let's Make a Wig

Creating a mane for a Snappy Lion or tufts of hair for a Snappy Squirrel is not as difficult as it might seem. Begin by tracing the wig pattern onto the back of a piece of long, shaggy mohair or faux fur. Make sure the fur is going in a downward direction. Follow the simple directions below. After you have made the wig it is easy to pull it onto the Snappy head.

Just cut the top curves 1/4 inch away from the sewing line.

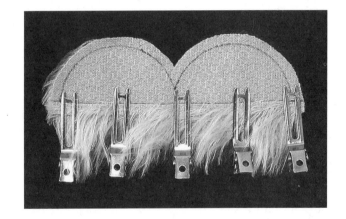

Fold up the bottom edge 1/4 inch and glue it down.

Fold the wig in half and pin the sides together.

Double sew the top curve for strength.

Trim the seam allowance to about 1/8 inch.

The Fashionable Snappy

Snappys are a stylish sort and love to find new ways to dress up. There are all sorts of ways to make colorful scarves. They can be sewn, knitted, or purchased from craft and doll shops.

The Snappy ears can be lined in bright colors or tiny print fabrics.

Snappy Bunny is wearing a lace ruff and rosebud buttons.

Snappy Bear is wearing a plaid suit with buttons.

Let's Make a Clown Ruff

There are several ways to make a gathered ruff for a Snappy to wear. Ribbons and lace trims are easy to turn into a ruff. Simply use a running stitch along one edge and gather into a circle.

You can create a double ruff by running a thin ribbon through the middle of a wide ribbon.

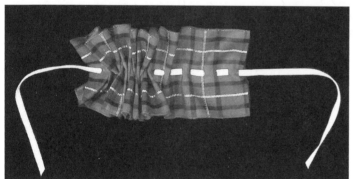

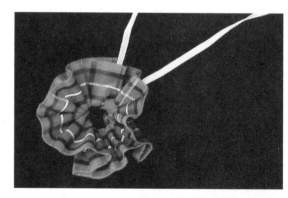

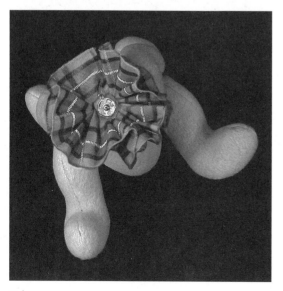

It is important to leave an opening for the head to attach to the body. Here is a trick to make the ruff fit around the Snappy's neck: Simply gather the fabric around a round object like a lipstick or thick marker and tie the ends together.

Woolen Scarf

Cut a piece of fabric 13 by 2 1/2 inches.

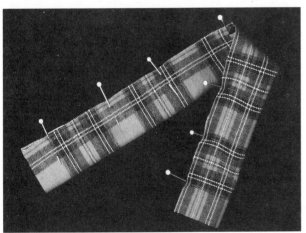

Fold the fabric in half lengthwise and pin the two sides together.

Sew a seam along the length of the scarf with 1/4 inch seam allowance.

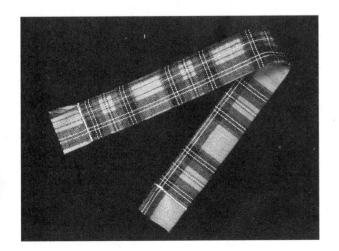

Turn out the scarf and sew a seam across one inch up from the end.

Use a needle to pull out the ends to create fringe.

Snappy Bear

These two bears love to wear plaid scarves and eat honey cookies at sunset.

Snappy Bear

Snappy Plaid Bear

This fashionable little bear dresses in a plaid outfit with a clown ruff and big buttons.

Snappy Plaid Bear

Snappy Bunny

These two bunnies enjoy carrots and searching for decorative eggs hidden in the garden.

Snappy Bunny

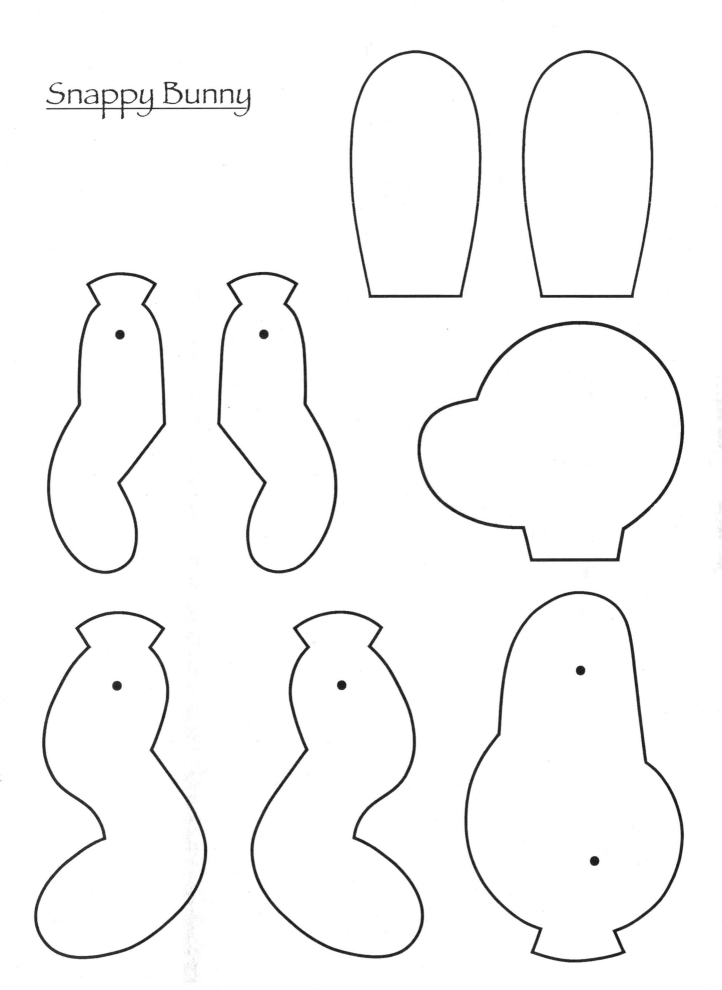

Snappy Elephant

This elephant would love to work in a circus with clowns who will feed him peanuts.

Snappy Elephant

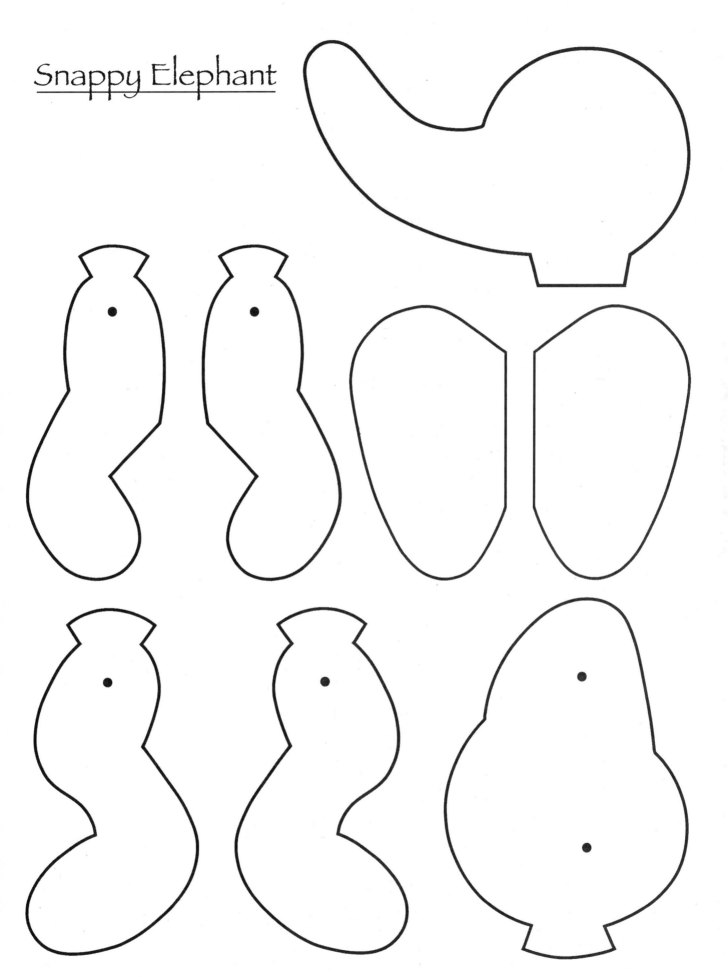

Snappy Hound

This hound dog enjoys sniffing around for hidden treasures to dig up and enjoy.

Snappy Hound

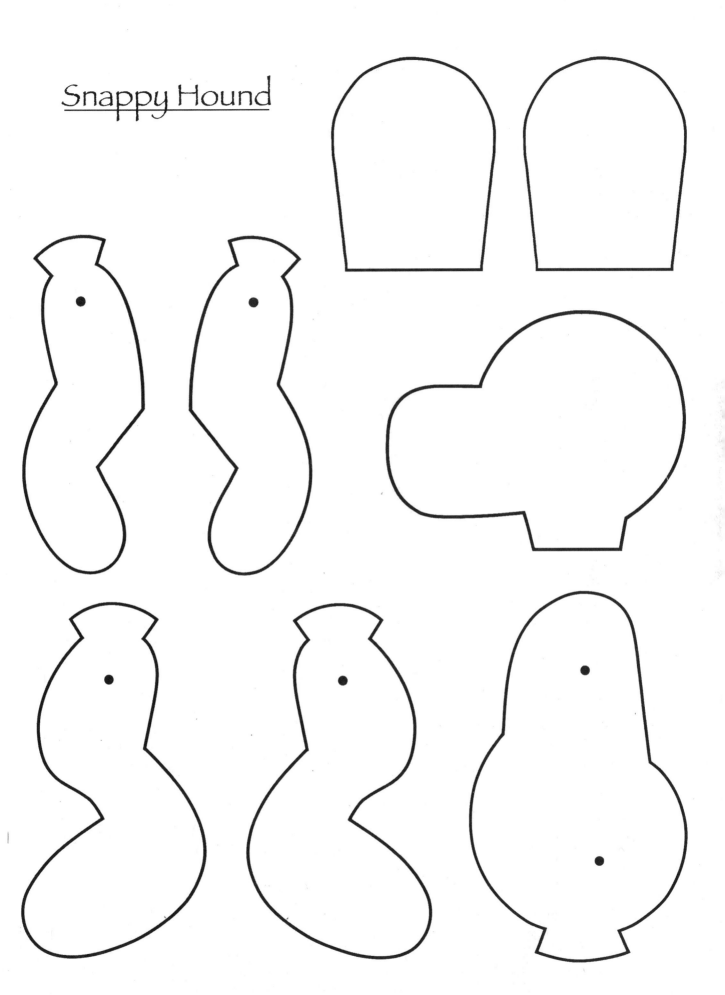

Snappy Lamb

This little lamb enjoys
giving wool to others to knit
a scarf or sweater.

Snappy Lamb

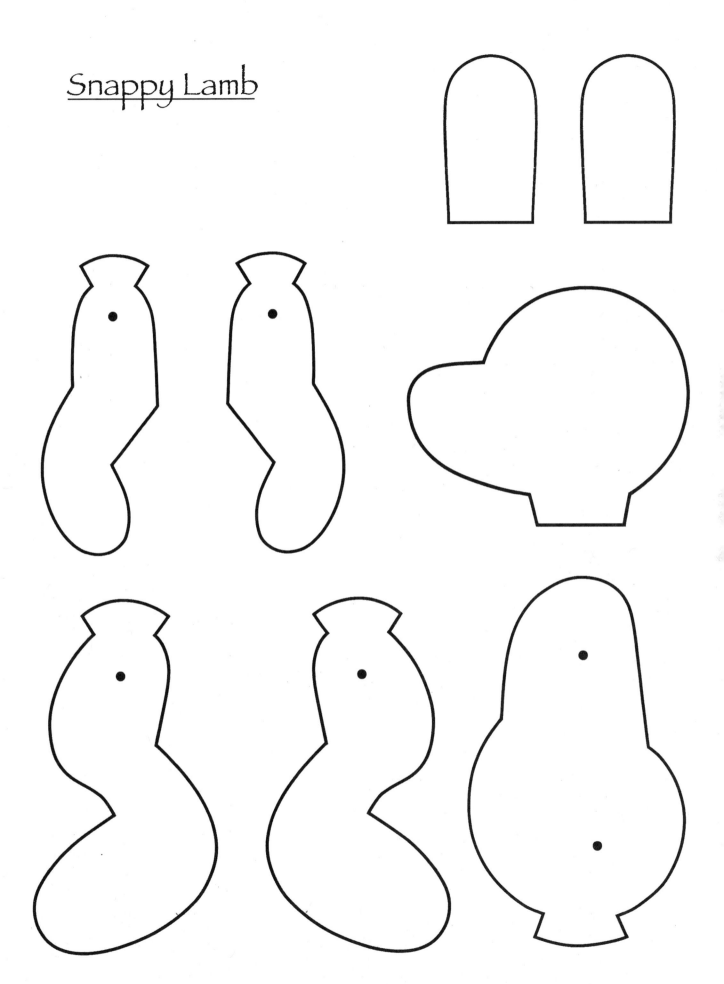

Snappy Lion

This lion enjoys
blueberries with
whipped cream and
roaring out loud with
laughter.

Snappy Lion

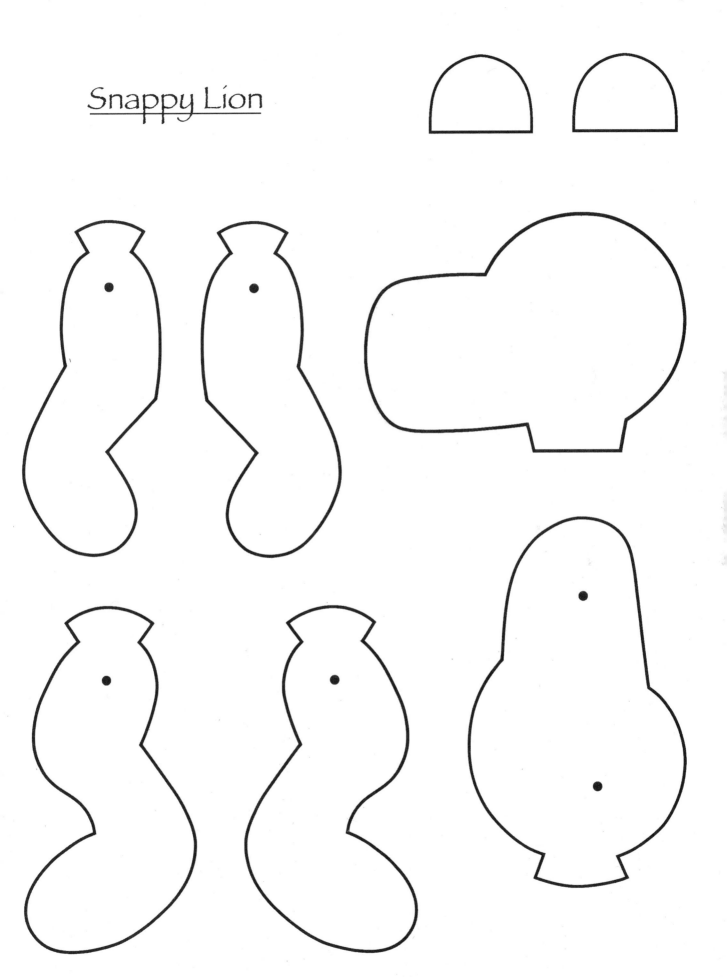

Snappy Mouse

This little mouse likes to scamper around the house looking for cheese.

Snappy Mouse

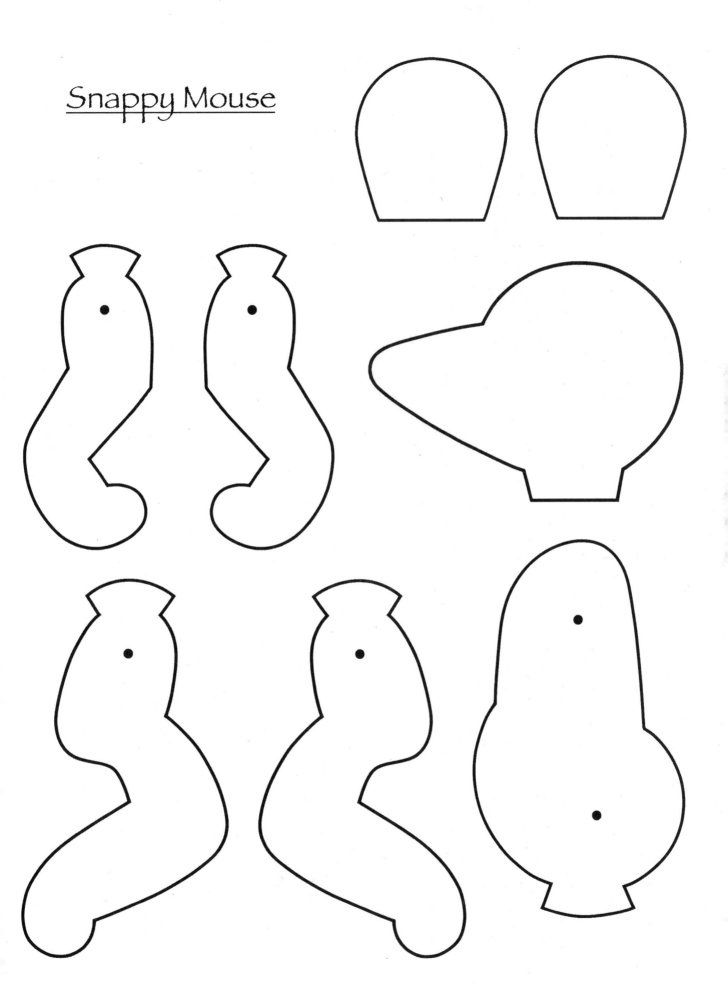

Snappy Panda

This panda is fond of bamboo dipped in honey at twilight when the moon is full.

Snappy Panda

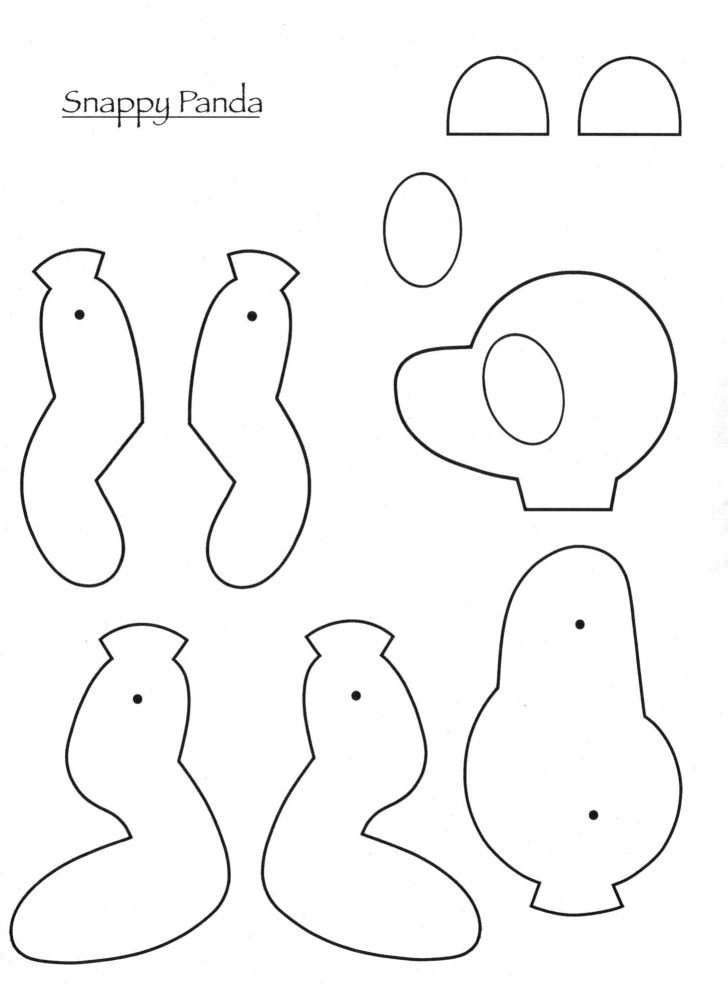

Snappy Puppy

This puppy enjoys a good bone and likes to bury them in the garden under the flowers.

Snappy Puppy

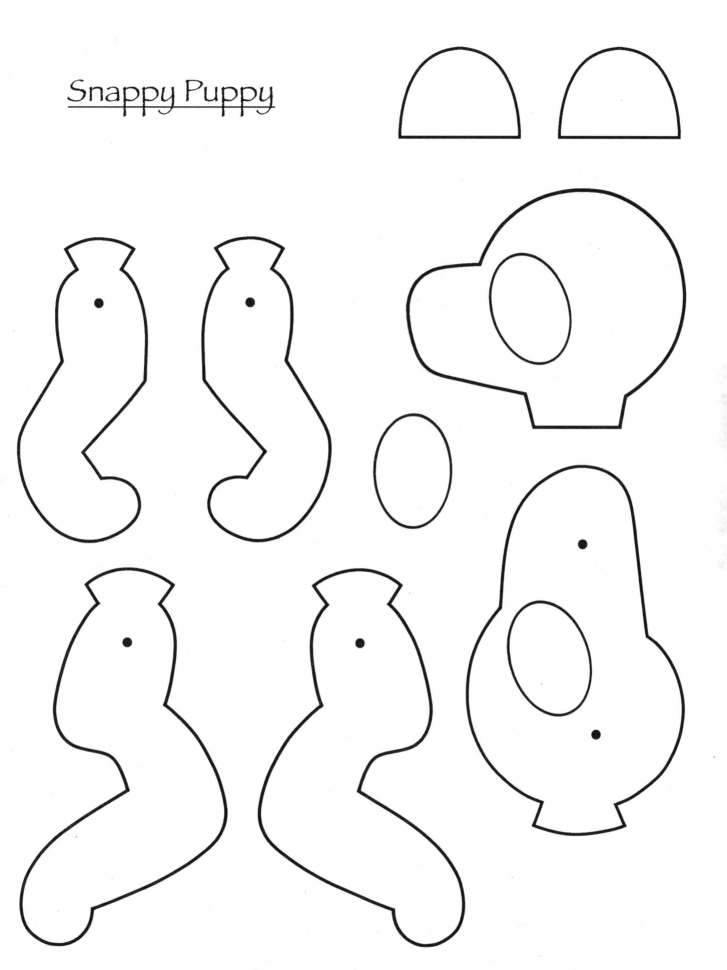

Snappy Reindeer

This red-nosed
reindeer loves to help
Santa deliver toys and
gifts to little children.

Snappy Reindeer

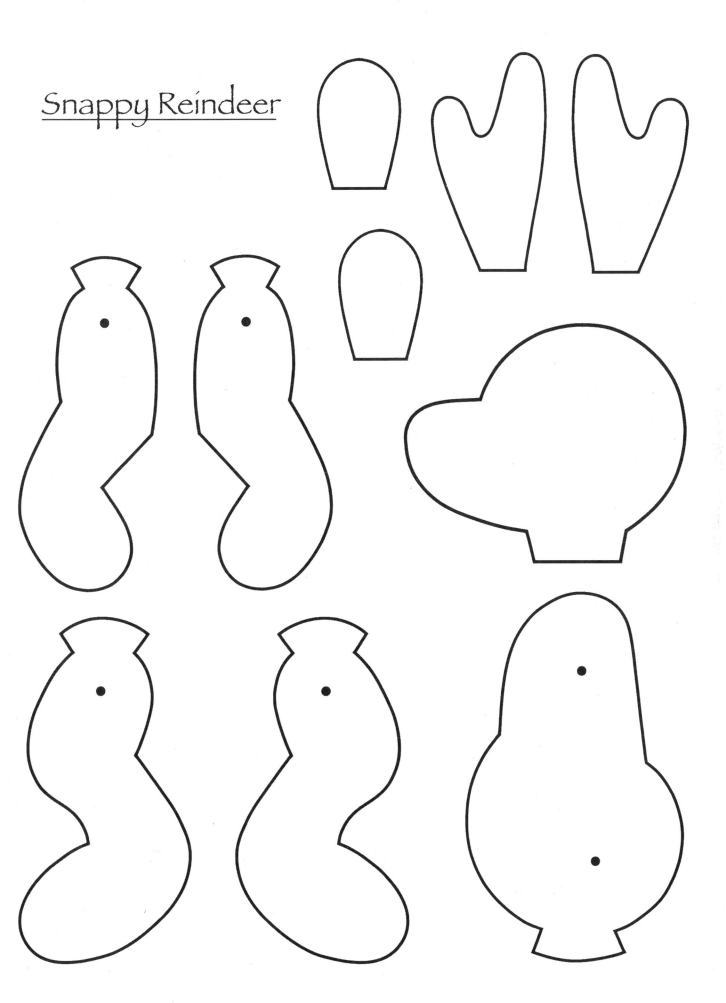

Snappy Siamese

This Siamese cat loves to take long walks in the forest looking for wild mushrooms.

Snappy Siamese

83

Snappy Squirrel

This squirrel stores acorns
and other nuts for winter
nights in front of the fire.

Snappy Squirrel

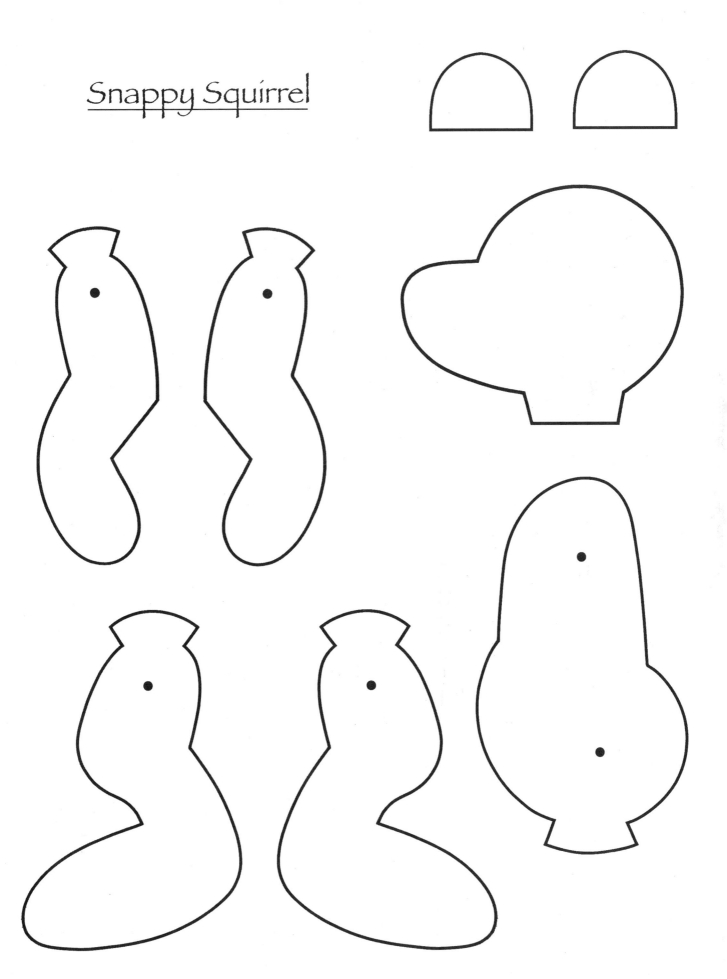

Snappy Tiger

These two tigers are cousins. One lives in the jungle and the other is a house cat.

Snappy Tiger

Heads & Tails

Here are the patterns for the Snappy wigs and tails.

The bunny, lamb, puppy, and reindeer can use a pom-pom for a tail.

The lion's tail is a tube of fabric with a fur tip.

You can use a pipe cleaner inside to add shape.

Adding a tail can give a Snappy even more personality!

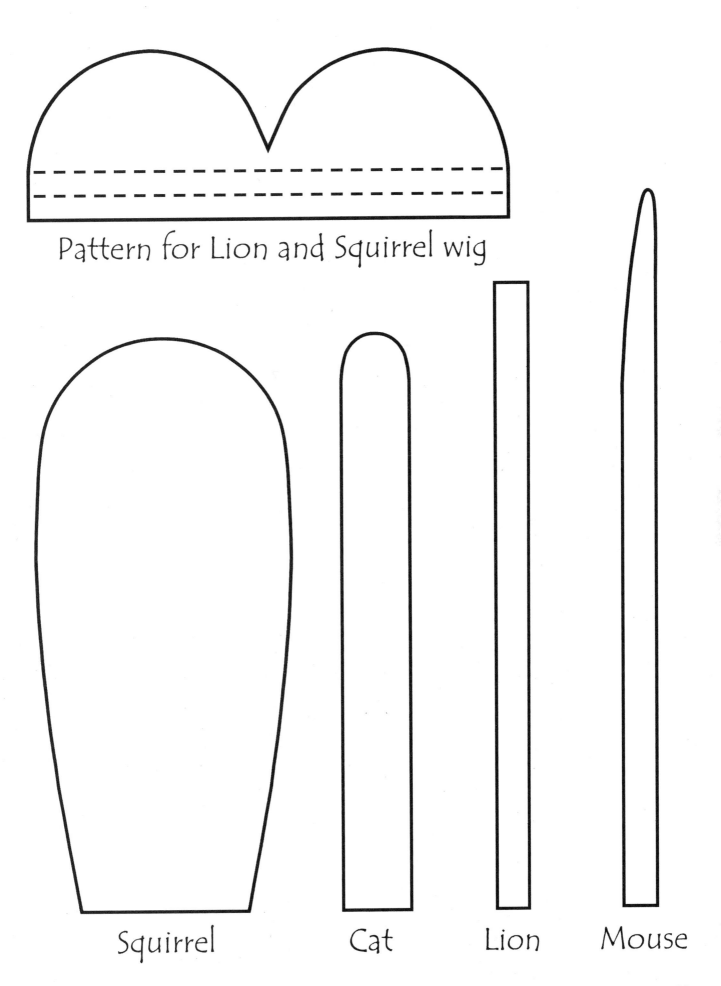

Pattern for Lion and Squirrel wig

Squirrel   Cat   Lion   Mouse

Snappy Accessories

Snappys love to have toys and accessories to play with. Here are patterns to make a bone, a heart, and a star. These are basic profile patterns that can be sewn, stuffed, and closed the same way as a Snappy. They can be made of various fabrics and decorated with a bit of imagination.

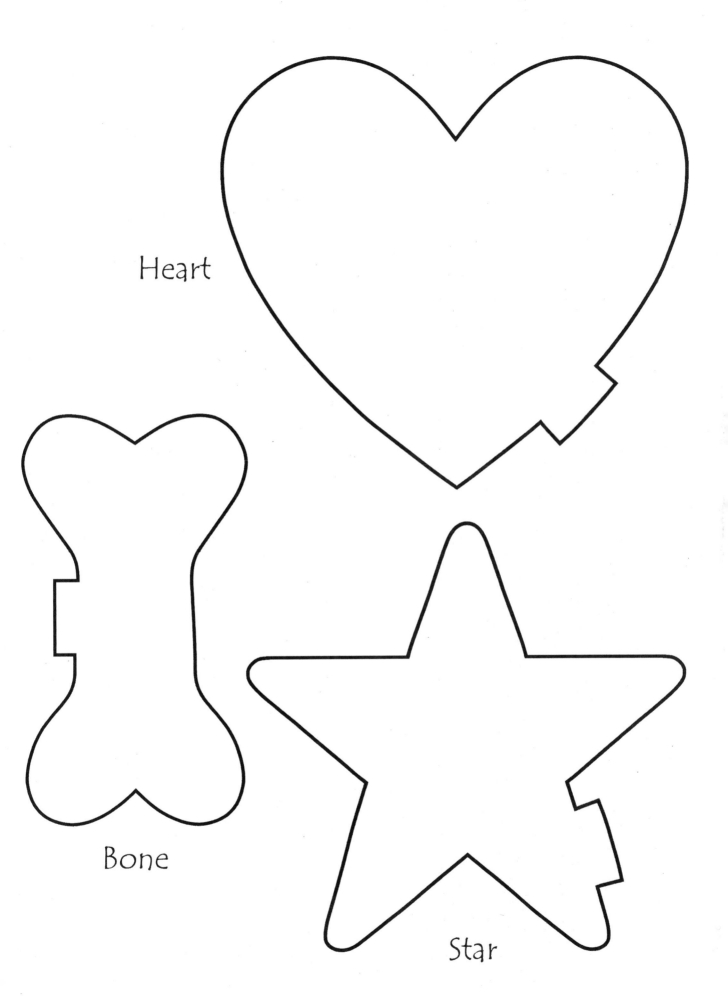

Heart

Bone

Star

Snappy Accessories

Snappys love to have toys and accessories to play with. Here are patterns to make an egg, a pumpkin, and an acorn. These are basic profile patterns that can be sewn, stuffed, and closed the same way as a Snappy. They can be made of various fabrics and decorated with a bit of imagination.

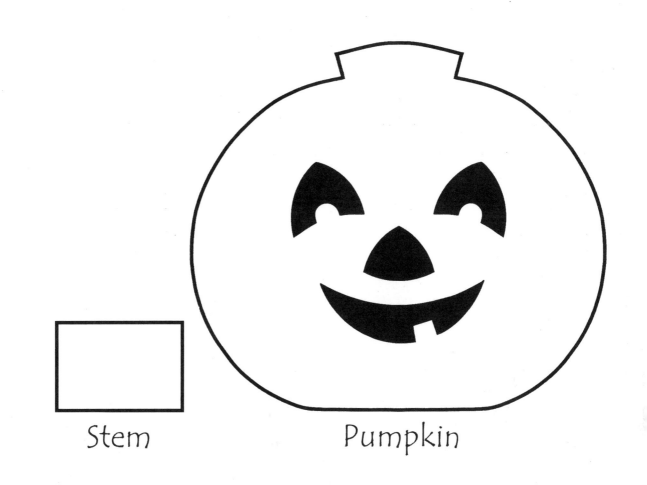

Stem   Pumpkin

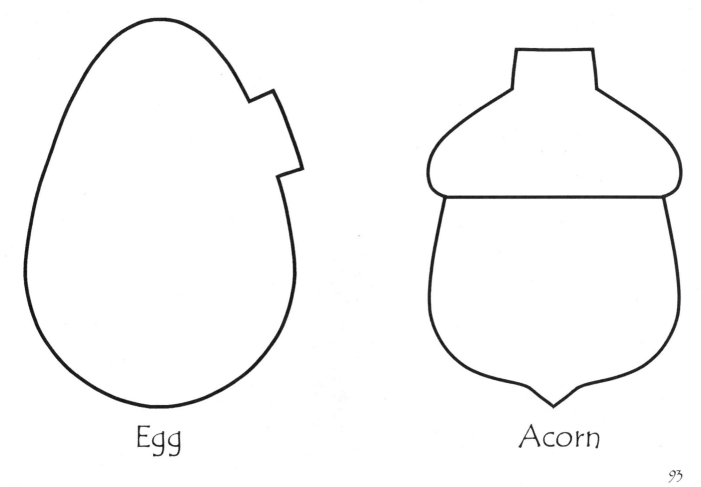

Egg   Acorn

93

Snappy Accessories

Snappys love to have toys and accessories to play with. Here are patterns to make a carrot, a shamrock, and a stocking. These are basic profile patterns that can be sewn, stuffed, and closed the same way as a Snappy. They can be made of various fabrics and decorated with a bit of imagination

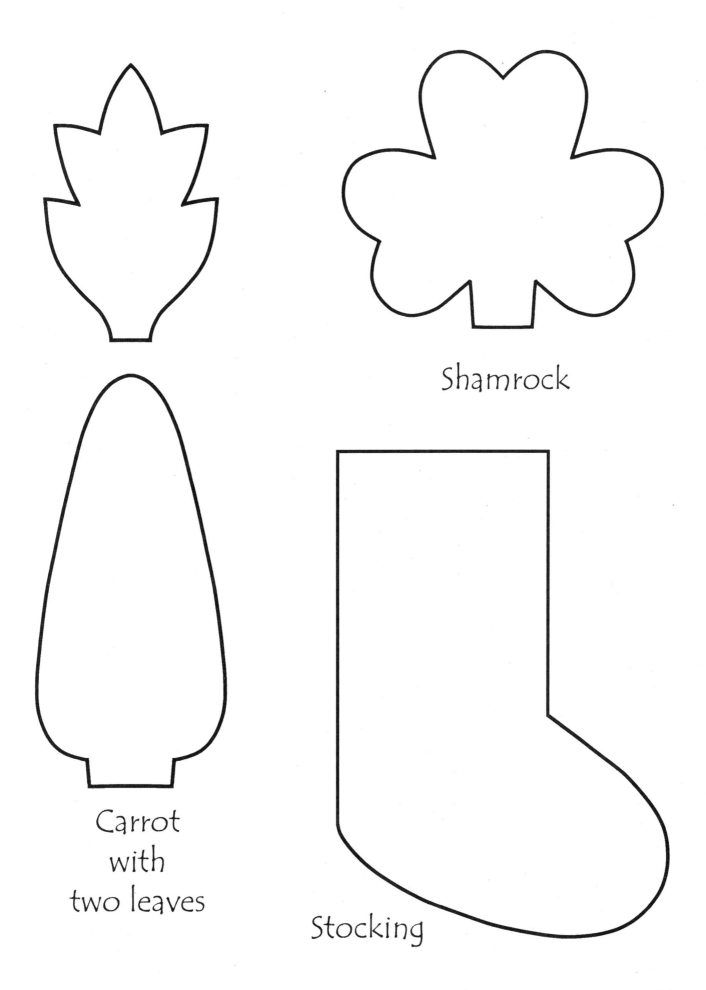

Shamrock

Carrot
with
two leaves

Stocking

Snappy Resources

The tools and materials that you will need to create your Snappys are available in most craft and fabric shops.

These days, many people shop online and that can be an even easier way to find what you will want for your Snappy project.

eBay is an amazing source for bundles of felt squares in a variety of colors and weights. There are also eBay sellers offering fleece and tiny beads for eyes. Online craft suppliers offer bags of multi-colored pom-poms in a wide range of colors.

The only fabric not generally available in craft and fabric shops, or on eBay is mohair, which is generally only available from a small number of importers. There is one company that offers a large selection of mohair from both England and Germany, as well as all the tools and threads you might need. They have outstanding customer service that is always helpful. So, if you decide to make a mohair Snappy the place to check out is Intercal Trading Group at http://www.intercaltg.com/.

ENJOY.